UNSHAKEABLE

"Embracing Faith in God Amid Adversity"

By

Darren D. Antonio, Sr.

Published by Distinction Publishing House
Dover, Denver, Colorado
United States of America
www.distinctionpublishinghouse.com

ISBN: 979-8-9894214-9-7

This book is printed on acid-free paper.

Printed in the United States of America

Dedication

This book is dedicated to people who desire to know Christ, trust in Christ, and believe that no matter what they experience on their journeys in life, Almighty God is always present, goes before, makes the path straight and guides every step.

This book is dedicated to you as you journey in life.

Acknowledgements

Special thanks to my beautiful, loving and supportive wife, Colette, who has been my typist, working tirelessly to compile this book to transmit to Sherry Johnson Deal, the editor, and Distinction Publishing House, the Publisher.

Special thanks are also extended to my two children, my daughter, Da'Renique and my son, Darren, Jr., for all their love and support.

Foreword

Unshakeable is a remarkable glimpse into the journey and constant battle we sometimes find ourselves in. We seek to find purpose amidst the chaos as we navigate the many issues, one after the other, that plague our existence from childhood through adulthood. Darren Antonio, Sr., having faced so many of life's bumps and turns, examines and surrenders to the "Author and Finisher of his faith," who took the broken pieces of what he thought was unrepairable, mended and saved his life.

Through scriptures, trusting and relying on God's promises, he allowed God to transform his brokenness, which was filled with carnal addiction, deceptiveness, sinful ways, weakness, suffering, and dysfunctional living to see meaning and purpose eventually.

In Unshakeable, Darren exposes the readers to his life story, highlighting those moments of uncertainty, trials, and periods of despair where he questioned his existence and what he did wrong to deserve such a fate. He provides solutions on how to navigate through the rocky mountains, deep plains and uncharted waters of life to find your why. He also highlights his transformation and the answers he obtained via four means: his unquenchable thirst for God, his quest for knowledge, the sixty-six books all rolled into one bestseller - the BIBLE, and the faith he gained in being consistent and persistent in God's love. Same can provide clarity, understanding, hope, guidance, inspiration, direction and solutions to every problem we could ever face on life's journey.

Unshakeable was written for those readers who need inspiration through their trials, reassurance that God is real, perspective on life's journey, and understanding that challenges are inevitable. Still, we do not have to face them alone. We have God, our captain, who has promised to be our present "help in times of trouble" and who has provided the Bible, a blueprint or roadmap for walking, navigating and recalibrating on our destined paths. We also have our faith even when we cannot see clear skies to transport us through high seas and unprecedented winds in the storms of life.

Colette B. Antonio, JP

Table of Contents

Introduction

After having to acquire the faith of Job and continue to believe and trust in my awesome maker, the great God Almighty, I have been convicted to put pen to paper and introduce to you my writing publicly. If you have not already gathered, the purpose behind writing this book is to inspire humanity, believers and non-believers to the recognition and existence of our great Creator and how sometimes trials and tribulations could lead one to seek Him.

Often during trials and tribulations, God nudges us to get our attention because He created us and wants us to know Him better. He loves His children and wants us to serve the purposes for which He ordained.

We often get distracted by the "Evil One" out here trying to kill, steal, and destroy. This is a true statement of how I had to battle with my Lord at the forefront, so that the "Wicked One" did not short-circuit my life prematurely on this earth.

In life, if we do not have a relationship with our Lord Jesus Christ, we make wrong decisions. We have to face the consequences. With freedom of choice comes responsibility. I grew up in the Roman Catholic Church, so I had some knowledge to go back to the foundation that I was grounded in to redeem myself and ask my Saviour not to take me off this earth prematurely.

It also allowed me to serve the purpose that He ordained me to fulfil. He loves us unconditionally and has extended His grace and mercies to us, so when we come to Him sincerely and ask for His forgiveness, He knows we are His children, and He pardons us.

From the day you were born until the day you die, especially if you repent and change your life for the Great God Almighty, He will continue to fight for you - tooth and nail, for your soul.

In this inspirational book, I will take you on a journey through my life to understand how life throws you certain curve balls and challenges because of our inability to discern people, their motives and agendas; as well as our behaviours, choices, how we accept, rise, and deal with challenges when navigating through life.

Through trials, sickness, faith, perseverance, determination and God's unmerited grace and mercies, I share how I continue to fight the devil tooth and nail with my awesome creator, the Great God Almighty.

He does not lose!

CHAPTER ONE

Life's Challenges

I was born on 22nd February, 1965, in Nassau, New Providence Island, the capital of the Commonwealth of The Bahamas. I lived on Brougham Street, a street off the main street, East Street, Over-The-Hill, near the city of Nassau. Brougham Street was my home for the first fourteen years of my life. It was considered a part of the "ghetto." I was the sixth of seven children in a single-parent home, where my mother ruled with authority.

As a timid child, I spent a lot of time internalising my feelings and pondering why I was here and the meaning of life. I never talked much, but was a very keen observer of my environment. All my life, I wrestled with many questions for God. I searched for answers, so I started searching in the Bible.

Life in the ghetto was easy for us because my mother sometimes worked two jobs, and we attended church regularly, never having time to be "caught up" in some of the social ills that affected residents of the ghetto.

Unfortunately, working two jobs and having seven children did not allow my mother time to give attention to all of her children. My eldest sister, Jay, took on that motherly role in her absence, which allowed me to grow very attached to her. I never was attached to my mother because I never felt that maternal bond that is usually established between a parent and child.

I considered myself the "black sheep" because I was less acknowledged and felt overlooked. I did not feel important. My mother had her favourite children, and she, to this day, still makes it known. I know parents have their favourites, but being so obvious about it can cause negative feelings to fester in the family among siblings. They try to make you feel not valuable, validated, and unimportant by saying negative things, etc.

I was and still am very outspoken because I do not believe in unfairness, favouritism, and bad-mouthing some of your children and praising others. I believe in being just and fair in my dealings with whomever I meet. When you are outspoken, you are viewed as being rude, even though you are correct. The older generation back then could not accept that. I do not hold any animosity towards my mother. I love her, and I will continue to pray that one day she will see the error of her ways.

Although we lived in the ghetto, we were not of the ghetto. This statement meant we lived there, but never behaved or associated with things and people that contributed to the social ills and problems in the ghetto. The neighbourhood comprised mixed ethnic backgrounds: Jamaicans, Haitians, Trinidadians, Guyanese, and Bahamians.

I was a fast learner. I believed in keeping my mouth shut and my eyes and ears open. This helped me to learn about my environment and the people around me, including my mother, grandmother, siblings, neighbours, etc. I did this all my life because I never took life casually. I learnt not to get involved in negative, destructive habits because they would take you down the wrong path. Some of my friends became involved in criminal activities, and thus, they eventually became regular criminals. My family always told us to avoid those types of friends to stay out of trouble and out of the policeman's hands.

We spent much time doing our sacraments at Our Lady's Catholic Church, which left no time to get involved in unscrupulous behaviours. I had a very active mind and always asked myself many questions, to which I sought answers.

I read my Bible intermittently, searching for answers as to why I was born and my reason or purpose for being on this earth. This had always been my daily task. As I read this excellent book, I found some answers as I continued my search. I was made in the image and likeness of God. According to Psalms 139:14-16, King David says, "I will praise you, for I am fearfully and wonderfully made; Marvelous are your works, and that my soul knows well. My frame was not hidden from you when I was made in secret and skillfully wrought in the lowest parts of the earth. Your eyes saw my substance, being yet unformed. And in your book, they all were written, the days fashioned for me, when as yet there were none of them." Also, according to 2 Corinthians 5:17, "Therefore, if anyone is in Christ, he is a new creation; old things have passed away; behold, all things have become new." So, I meditated on these verses and held on to them. My reason for searching for answers was that I continued to ask myself questions because some of the things I observed and was taught made little sense.

I grew up in a family that was divided. There was always tension and strife. Peace was a foreign word and rarely existed in my home. One question that haunted me was why I never met my father. There was no conversation or intention to talk about his identity or information about him. He was a figment of my imagination, and as I would come to realize who he was, like everything else, was a secret. I could not ask or inquire about such details at the time because it would have had serious consequences. There was always an element of fear present, so I was reluctant to inquire to avoid any verbal repercussions. I was very aware of what I could say at that age. I was wise enough to solicit bits and pieces of information from my eldest sister, Jay, who after I enquired was open to updating me on specific details. I got the information with relative ease.

I learned how the family interacted with each other, their beliefs in certain things, their views on certain aspects of life, and how the children were viewed regarding their importance. As for me, I was the sixth of seven children and sometimes felt as if I was the least important of us all. It was not very encouraging, but I was a fighter. I am one of those rare people who, when I am viewed as the least important, it causes me to become dogged in my views and focus more on God's word because I know He has never placed any restrictions on my life, and with Him, "all things are possible." I knew I was created in his image, and I never saw myself as less than anyone else, regardless of who I am or anyone else's opinion of me.

In all of this, I have realized, according to the book of Jeremiah Chapter 1:15 of the Old Testament, "God knew us before he formed us in the womb." This scripture tells me that regardless of the circumstances surrounding me coming to be here, the great God Almighty has strategically placed me on this earth, where I grew up, with a specific purpose in mind. We are all created in His image and likeness, and for me, that settles that. Jeremiah 29:11 says, "For I know the thoughts that I think toward you, saith the Lord, thoughts of peace, and not of evil, to give you an expected end."

At a young age, I was plagued with medical issues. As I grew up, what became very troubling to me was that all my siblings were healthy, and I was the one diagnosed with chronic asthma. On my mother's side, none of my siblings had asthma. As for my father's side, I did not know his medical history because as stated earlier, I did not know him and discussing him was an off-limits subject. Why was I the only child living this miserable life? Why was I the only one bearing this cross? I felt like someone had punched me in the gut.

Why am I faced with this miserable life? This was the question I usually asked myself. Asthma is not only a nuisance, but it terrorizes your life. You cannot play the type of sports that you like - basketball, track & field and a host of recreational things that can cause you to exert yourself. A chronic or acute asthmatic has to monitor how he or she plays sports because too much exertion may result in an asthmatic attack.

As I grew, my asthma worsened, and I became frightened, worried, and perplexed. I practically lived in Princess Margaret Hospital (PMH), almost daily. This is the Bahamas' Public Hospital, which most people went to because it was free of charge to the poor citizenry.

I was introduced to various bush medicines (Aloes, Cerasee, Croton, Soursop, and Kamalame). These were used to cure my asthma and a few others that my mother tried. I grew. My height was measured alongside a tree. Measuring a child with asthma to a tree is one of the things Bahamians do because it is said that once you do this, as the tree grows, the child grows out of asthma. This was done, but it did not work.

I read a lot of healing verses in the Bible as the asthma got worse, trying to find answers to what was happening in my life. For me, it was a battle almost daily to stay alive. The pain was very unbearable. When you cannot breathe, there are no words to describe the pain that you face; it feels as though the air is being squeezed out of you, which suffocates the life out of you.

In my opinion, this is only a mild description of the gravity of the situation when faced with such a traumatic experience. I asked myself and my God what have I done to deserve such a miserable life. I cried many times, and I reached out to my God never to leave me nor forsake me because I could not carry this burden by myself at times. I was really depressed, but I was not giving up.

Being unable to breathe is a death sentence for anyone, and there I was in a constant battle for my life. I started thinking if this was some curse on me, especially knowing that I was the only child carrying this burden and not knowing my medical history on my father's side of the family. I read up on generational curses and wondered if my fore parents, mother, father, or grandfather had dabbled or placed their hands in something ungodly that was causing me to pay the price. It made me very concerned because the obstacles became more frequent and life-threatening.

I attended William Gordon Primary School, D. W. Davis Junior High School, and the great Government High School (GHS). Throughout my schooling, I was plagued with this disease. I was weary and sometimes practically out of breath during my exams. I did examinations at D. W. Davis, Bahamas Junior Certificates and at GHS, General Certificate of Education, a London-based examination. I was successful in my BJCs and my GCEs even though I wrestled with not being able to breathe properly when I sat my exams. During the exams, I prayed they would end soon so I could go to PMH for some relief.

Occasionally, immediately after exams, I had to go directly to PMH. I continued to fight for my life because, at times, I thought I would not live that long because of the frequency and seriousness of my asthma attacks, but this was just the beginning of my troubles and trials.

Somehow, during these battles, I fought for my life for as long as possible. I told myself this would be a daily battle because I had just arrived and was not ready to leave. I continued to read and search my Bible, and I gained faith in God by reading it. I quoted healing scriptures like Psalms 107:19-20 which says, "When we call out to you, the eternal one, you will give the order, heal and rescue us from sudden death." When you continue to build your faith in the Lord Jesus Christ, there is no sickness He cannot heal because He is our healer, miracle worker, and everything. I know that He will break the power of sickness out of my life if I repent, turn my life over to Him, and serve Him for the rest of the days that He grants me on this earth. He has helped me to be an overcomer, but I had to build faith in Him by reading His Word daily.

Also, I read other scriptures like Jeremiah 33:6 says, "But now, I will heal and mend them. I will make them whole and bless them with abundant peace and security." Please, Father, let your word be fulfilled in my life. My confidence grew in Him, and I continued and decided that this would be a fight for my life and that if I was going down, it would not be without a fight. This meant war.

This life was the life of Darren D'Angelo Antonio, someone who had fought the devil tooth and nail, battling for life with the help of Jesus Christ, my Saviour, who did all the work. I continue to give Him all the praise, glory for still being alive and enjoying life to this day. My Saviour, Jesus Christ, is fantastic, compassionate, empathetic, all-loving, merciful, and full of grace. He is my healer, my source, and the strength I needed when I thought I had none.

As I matured and learned about God, His son, Jesus Christ, and the Holy Spirit, I became committed to studying the Word and getting to know them better. This was no game, but the more I read the Bible, I think Satan got vexed because his attacks became more frequent, and my life was in balance. Sometimes faith, hope and rest fluctuated with fear, despair, and the attacks, and I had to deal with them individually. When you are dealing with fear, it is of the devil, it is demonic, and it has the tendency to paralyse you, and you have to be equipped with the armour of the Lord to be geared up for this fight. You have to be battle-ready and fully attired for warfare prayer. It was as if he was trying to kill me. I was in PMH almost daily.

Daily, I had to take an intravenous "IV" of aminophylline, hydrocortisone 500 mg and an oxygen mask to try to breathe. I just about lived in the emergency room of PMH every week for a few days until the doctors decided to admit me to the Male Medical Ward "MMW," or sometimes the Intensive Care Unit "ICU," depending on the severity of my condition.

The Lord God was at the front of my battles, and I was not giving up. My mental state at the time was very depressing, and at times, I became disillusioned because some of my brief, healthy moments did not last long. Many times, on the Ward, I watched people die around me, but giving up was not an option. I told the Lord; I am with you, and you cannot lose any battle, which is how I reassured myself to stay confident sometimes.

Over those years, I had been in PMH about twenty times on a ventilator in the ICU. This became my everyday life. I was also aware of people dying around me in the ICU over the years. I cried to the Lord many times to relieve me from this burden so I could live an everyday life like my siblings because it was so much for me to bear.

I was not looking for self-pity, but was asking and looking for healing. Sometimes, my mind was in turmoil, and I was baffled about what was happening in my life and if I could ever live a healthy and everyday life like my siblings. I believed in God and had faith, but it was being built incrementally, and I had to continue to pray and study God's Word.

I attended school as much as I could. I had a decent attendance record, but I often wheezed. This disease was not letting up or giving me a break. Despite my daily battles with this disease, it was not giving me a break.

In my neighbourhood, young teenagers' males and some females started smoking marijuana. Teenage pregnancy was increasing, and crime was on the rise. The Haitian Voodoo Man was in demand. The area began to change culturally, and my mother, unknown to me, was looking to move out of the site to avoid us from being caught up in that way of life.

One weekend night, my mother moved us out of the neighbourhood around 3:00 a.m. We were reluctant to leave, but it was for our good. We moved into Nassau Village Subdivision, referred to as "The Village," a neighbourhood in the eastern area of the Island. There, we would live for the next nine years. In the village, I had some of the worst experiences with asthma, and more severe battles were on the way.

My eldest brother, Ricky, had a vehicle, but as a Bahamas Customs Officer, he worked practically night and day. When I got an asthma attack, we had to wait for a friend to pass by before I could get a ride to PMH. At times, when it became too late, my family would call an ambulance. For some reason, calling the ambulance was the last resort, regardless of my worsening condition.

Several times, I had to walk, whether in the morning or noon, from the back road to the bus stop at the village entrance and Soldier Road. I would get on the bus, not able to breathe correctly. My Ventolin inhaler and I would get dropped off on Shirley Street opposite PMH. I would walk across the street safely when the traffic cleared and up the hill to PMH. Steps away in PMH yard, I took my time, stopping along the way to catch my breath before continuing to the emergency room "ER." When I arrived at the ER, I was out of breath and ready to collapse from exhaustion. Only by the grace of Almighty God was I able to reach PMH on all occasions. This was a constant battle for me. Depression at times set in, and I felt helpless. I became slightly depressed, trying to catch my breath and hold on to my faith because of a lack of oxygen in my brain.

Asthma and hospital combination weighed mentally and emotionally on me and my family, but I would not give up. I was learning about God. I was back and forth with my faith, but it was not strong enough. Throughout this battle, I realised that there were two choices in life. You have free will, but it comes with conditions set in stone. You either accept God's commandments and the "free gift of salvation" and live eternally or reject it and let that other fellow, Satan, own your soul. He would take you into eternal damnation.

I learned about this other fellow from the Bible. It told me he was out here killing, stealing, and destroying humanity with no remorse because he already knew his verdict. He does not go on holiday. He is constantly in attack mode. He used to live in heaven and sing in the halls of the Lord, lighting up heaven, but he allowed sin to creep into his heart and became prideful. He tried to ascend above God, His creator, which was how all hell broke loose. He was one of the Lord's favourite creations, but pride overcame Him, which caused Him and one-third of the angels to be kicked out of heaven. Since then, he has been on a rampage, trying to run competition and oppose everything our creator has done. Now, He is who we must battle. Fortunately, we have our creator, God Almighty, to fight our battles against him.

While living in the village, I finished junior and senior high school despite my constant medical battles. When I had completed high school, I worked respectively at a food store, at our national water company, at the Bahamas Department of Corrections as a correctional officer, and on 4th January, 1988 at Bahamas Electricity Corporation (BEC), where I have been employed after thirty-five years. At times, I could manage my chronic asthma, but it was a little less frequent but more severe. I was given just about every remedy that my mother could lay her hands on. I took the Aloes plant regularly, drank Croton tea, and took medications in rotation: Prednisone, Ventolin inhaler, and Ventolin tablets. Also, the house had not to be dusty, and my area had no animals like cats or dogs or any hearty animals.

CHAPTER TWO
Understanding Life's Lessons

In October of 1989, my life took a strange turn. I met a young lady whom I would call Susan. We were involved in a two-year relationship. She was my first girlfriend. Despite my medical battles, I had goals set for my life – being in a relationship at that time was not one of them. I was determined to accomplish my goals. Susan had two children and was experienced, and I was inexperienced and naïve.

On that rainy day in October of 1989, I was travelling with her brother, whom I will call John. I met John at The Bahamas' Her Majesty's Prison. He was my squad mate, and we became friends, getting to know each other through employment. We became even closer when I got involved with his sister, Susan. John decided to stop by his sister Susan's apartment. When we arrived there, he knocked on the door; she opened it, and we entered the apartment. John introduced me to Susan and his other sister, Maria, and informed them who I was.

This was the beginning of our two-year relationship and a very interesting one for me. As time went on, we became very close. She became my girlfriend. Our lives were moving very fast. That night, I met Susan; she cooked some pork chops and white rice in the kitchen. When the food was finished, she took some food for John, Maria, and herself. She asked if I wanted some, but I declined because I was taught never to eat from people.

After her siblings had eaten, they laid down on the living room floor a short while later and went to sleep. As time passed, the rain came down, pouring like a hurricane. Susan went into the bathroom to take a bath, and I was left sitting in the living room watching the World Series baseball game between the San Francisco Giants and the Oakland Athletics.

After bathing, Susan came out of the bathroom wearing a black bra and a slip. She came to me and said, "John and Maria are sleeping, and she has a television in her room, and I can watch the game from there." I thought nothing out of the ordinary, so I joined her. I went inside her room, and she turned on the television. I sat in the chair, and she lay on the bed. At this time, I tried to remain focused on the baseball game, but she struck up a conversation about my job and how I got to know her brother, John. The conversation switched to relationships between watching the television and conversing with her. Susan was fascinating and asked me many personal questions and whether I was involved in any relationship. I was still focusing on the World Series and talking with Susan.

During our conversation, I tried to continue watching my baseball game, but after I harmlessly, not aware of the consequences of my response, mentioned to her I was still a virgin, she moved closer to me and looked me directly in the eyes. Our eyes were locked for a moment without blinking. I felt paralysed. The only thing that caught my senses was her perfume, which lingered heavily in the room. A soft, sweet, and fragrant scent that captivated my senses. The room was neatly decorated with everything in its place, a small yet cosy setting. It was overly quiet except for the game on the television, which she got up and turned the volume down very low. The room was also dark except for the light that beamed from the television, which cascaded various shades of light and then darkness as the pictures changed on the screen. She gently undressed me. I was completely helpless as she continued to strip me naked. She kissed me on my lips, neck, chest, and I became weak and gave in to her advances. She was gentle. Although I did not want to say it, I enjoyed every moment.

Honestly, after I mentioned I was still a virgin, everything happened so fast that I did not initially grasp the gravity of what had happened. One minute, I was watching television and talking; the next, we were intimately involved. When everything was over and done with, and I went home, reality and guilt overwhelmed me.

I was stunned because I promised to save myself for my wife when I got married. I did not arrive home until midnight because of the heavy rain and having to wake John up to take me home. When I arrived at the time, I got inside the house. I had to explain to my mother where I was coming from at this hour and who those people were who dropped me home. After explaining to my mother how I was stuck in the rain with John by his sister Susan's apartment and waiting for the rain to subside so I could get home, she was pleased, and I went to bed.

I went to bed, but I could not sleep. I felt guilty losing my virginity to someone who was not my wife. All my life, I had promised myself that I would save myself for my wife when I married. I had no shuteye because a car horn blew outside my home at six o'clock. It was a long, stretched white limousine. My mother's bedroom was at the front of the house. She was calling me to see who was blowing their horn in her yard that early in the morning.

I went outside, and as I approached the limo, I did not recognise the driver, but he told me to look inside the back seat, and there was Susan stretched out in the back seat, smiling. She said she came for me and told me the driver was her brother, Ben, who worked for the limo company. I told Susan I could not go with her because it was too early in the morning. I told her that sometime that evening, I would visit her. She was reluctant, and she left without me.

I saw Susan that evening, and we talked about various things. During the conversation, she told me she had two sons, Brian and Robert, who had the same father. After that first encounter, it almost seemed as though it was spellbinding when I got in her presence. There was a heightened sense of physical and sexual attraction because after that, the constant physical attraction of the flesh dominated my thoughts and our relationship. It became a point where I felt as if I had no control and the more we spent time together, the more we got lost in ecstasy.

Although I initially wanted to save myself for marriage, it was over from the first time I met Susan. Susan had an extremely high sex drive, and every time I was in her presence or talking on the telephone, she told me she could not get enough of me. Making love regularly was the order of the day or the night.

As I got to know Susan better, I realised she was a fatal attraction with low self-esteem. She worked for the major airline, Bahamasair, as an agent. I was so engulfed in this relationship that I became addicted. Every time we were in each other's presence, we ended up naked, and I was too powerless to resist; I could not help myself.

Susan was so jealous of other women coming near me or talking to me, and she became furious if I was talking to a female co-worker at my job. She would be in the parking lot waiting for me to get off sometimes and she would see us walking, talking, and heading towards our respective vehicles that came to pick us up from work. Still, when I would pick her up from work, her male and female co-workers were talking, and I did not get mad because I was mature enough to understand that it was normal to converse with your co-workers, male or female.

I observed Susan for six months, her cursing when speaking, her bad attitude, and her bossy ways. One Sunday afternoon, I went to her apartment, sat her down on her bed, and decided to talk with her about her attitude.

After living in the village for nine years, we moved to Winton Meadows Subdivision "Winton," further east in Nassau. I lived in Winton with my mother and some of my siblings. Susan lived on the central part of the island of Nassau. Susan moved from her address in central Nassau to Lumumba Lane, around the corner from where I lived out east.

I rode a racer bicycle to work when I first met Susan, but she owned a car, and she picked me up from work as often as she could because it appeared that she never wanted me out of her sight. She also loaned me her car so that, to my thinking, I would always have to come back to her. I worked shifts from eight to four, four to twelve and twelve to eight. One Sunday afternoon, I went to her to sit down and talk with her. I explained that I do not row, fight, curse or disrespect women. I told her that if she and I would continue our relationship, she had to change her behaviour. I told Susan that I have no tolerance for that type of behaviour.

I told her that if she did not change her behaviour, I would immediately remove myself from this relationship. I did not expect her to change overnight, but I expected her to make an attempt to change her actions in a reasonable time. I saw some significant changes within a few months, but from there she went in another direction.

Susan convinced me to sleep in her apartment, and I was persuaded. Apart from working shifts, I had never slept out of my mother's home. Susan had convinced and taken control of me, and I had agreed. I would sleep from Monday to Thursday at home, and Friday to Sunday belonged to Susan and me. I still spent time with Susan from Monday to Thursday every day of the week. Susan would take her two sons and drop them off by her mother, and we could spend the weekend sometimes at her apartment or in Miami because she got tickets at low prices, so we would alternate weekends.

Despite Susan trying to keep a tight leash on me, I met a Christian lady named Margo. Margo and I became involved. She was a loving, God-fearing, sweet lady who showed me genuine love. As I got to know her more and more each day, I grew to love her. I got to know her family well, and they accepted me as their son-in-law. We used to go out regularly and have picnics on Sundays on the beach, and I often had dinner with her family. I was between Susan and Margo, but I was immature and naïve with Susan, and I did not realise how dangerous she was.

Margo and I became very close, and we were talking about marriage off and on seriously. My mother was not in favour of Susan. She made it known to me. One day, she called Margo and told her everything about my double life, which hurt me dearly. Margo asked me about the little time I spent with her, but I would lie about how I spent my time. Little did I know, my mother and sister Debbie had told her everything about Susan and me, and they also took Margo to where Susan lived and showed her the apartment. I was lying to Margo, but she knew the truth. She pretended like she did not know.

I continued to see Susan, and we were still deeply involved. I tried to manage both relationships simultaneously. On the one hand, I was enjoying Susan's pleasures of the flesh; on the other hand, I was looking at Margo as my potential wife.

As time went on, I was able to save and purchase a very nice Oldsmobile Ciera from Ride Motors in Miami, and I was so happy that I had finally purchased a car, but little did I know all hell would break loose.

I went to Margo and showed her my car, and she was extremely happy for me. Then she cried nonstop. She told me how she knew what I was doing and that my mother and sister Debbie told her everything about Susan. All the lies and betraying Margo deeply hurt me because I loved her. She said to me she knew where I was many nights and that she went to bed crying all night and woke up every morning with a soaked pillow.

I took Margo out on a date to convince her she was my girl and that I would stop seeing Susan. She told me she loved me and would like to make one request of me before I departed for home. I told Margo to tell me, and she said I must never let Susan drive my car, but she did not tell me why.

Margo was a praying young lady. That request still lives with me today. Considering what she told me, I left her that evening but still ended up with Susan. When I arrived at Susan's apartment and went inside, she was not pleased. I thought that with me working shift and now having my car, she would have been happy for me, but I was dead wrong.

Susan was not pleased with me buying a car, and when I arrived at her apartment, she practically tore off my clothes, and we shared some passionate, intimate moments in the living room.

Several days before my car came, I could recall finding some weird things in Susan's house. One afternoon, I was in her apartment while she was at work, and I found a white paper with a circle and white powder with my name written on it and a scary doll in the drawer. I waited until she came home from work, and then I took her straight to the back door, opened it, and showed her all her wicked Obeah stuff. She broke down crying and said that she loved me and that it would never happen again. The next day, I found more of her Obeah things, and I again made her burn them up, and she promised she would not do it again.

I brought my car to Susan to show it to her, but Susan was furious, unlike Margo, who was happy. Susan relaxed for a while and then engaged me that night, and we were intimately involved on two separate occasions.

While lying in bed, she relentlessly begged me to lend her my car because she needed to make a run somewhere. Susan intensified her begging and crying for me to lend her my car, nonstop. After all this begging and crying, I became emotionally exhausted, and I started to rationalise that she let me drive her own car with no problem, and that is why I should do the same for her. I ignored what Margo had told me, and it almost cost me my life. I do not drink, smoke, or go partying with the boys, and I am always sober-minded. If that run was so urgent and she did not have wicked intentions, she should have driven her own car. My car was crushed like a foil paper in somebody's hands. I loaned her my car, and she took it to the Obeah woman, and whatever that lady did to my vehicle wickedly resulted in my traffic accident.

I wish to digress here and talk about one Sunday afternoon. I went by Susan, and as I walked into the apartment, I saw a big plate of white rice and corned beef. We call this *"fire engine"* in The Bahamas, and this plate of food was sitting on the counter prepared for me to eat. Susan came towards me and told me it was my dinner. I was brought up never to eat from people. She has never cooked for me since I have been with her, and I found it very strange. I told her I had eaten at home and my stomach was full. Susan became extremely angry, picked up that plate of food, and smashed it against the wall. She went angrily to her bedroom. I quickly went behind her and asked what happened, what was wrong, and if I had done something to her. She started crying. I tried to console her, but to no avail.

I left the apartment, got on my bicycle, and started home. I was fed up with her insecurities. A few minutes later, as I was travelling on Fox Hill Road, headed east to my home, I heard this car behind me. There was Susan, still crying. She pulled beside me and begged me to return to the apartment. I did not look back and continued on my way home. I did not look back because I knew there was a sinister motive behind this plate of food. I told Susan before that whatever inadequacies or deficiencies that she had or how she felt about our relationship that I was not the person responsible for that. I was around her almost all day and all night when I was not working. The next day, she convinced me to come home to her apartment, apologised for her behaviour, and took me to Miami for the weekend.

On 1st July, 1990, that Saturday night, I placed my car keys in Susan's hand, and she left the apartment. When she returned about two hours later, her facial countenance was grave, and I could see she was still unhappy that I had bought my car. It was my money, and it was a necessity that I have my transportation because I was a shift worker and did not want to rely on anyone to get to and from work on time.

On Sunday, 2nd July of, 1990. I was dressed for work at 7:15 a.m., travelling down Yamacraw Hill Road, a street in the Eastern District of Nassau. I was headed to my job at the electrical company. I did not drink or smoke, and I was involved in a severe traffic accident. My vehicle, the Oldsmobile Ciera, was wrapped around one of those big trees by the Bahamas Prison, and that was the last thing I remembered. I was in a coma from 2nd July at around 7:15 a.m. until Friday, 7th July at about 9:00 p.m. If you had seen my car, you would have known that the only way I could have survived that accident was because of a miracle by the Almighty God.

On that Friday evening, I regained consciousness at about 9:00 p.m., and there was Margo beside me, crying and thanking God that I was still alive. I did not realise how serious the accident was until Margo told me. She prayed for me, and afterwards, she left; shortly after Margo left, Susan arrived. Here was Susan with no care or concern on her face and acting as if nothing had happened. I was perplexed because I did not comprehend how someone could claim to love you, but if they feel threatened by another rival, they would prefer to take your life with no remorse.

I went home from the hospital, still dating both ladies, and decided to plan how to fix or correct this situation with both Susan and Margo. It was not a matter of knowing whom I wanted or who was best for me, but it was about how I would get rid of Susan. Here I was, still having dinner with Margo's family like the favourite son-in-law and battling the powerful sex stronghold that Susan had on me. I figured out why I could not break away from Susan. Once I was in Susan's presence, regardless of what I was saying to myself, I would not give in, but I was powerless when I was in her presence.

In the car accident, I received one broken finger on my right hand next to the pinky finger, a laceration on my lower right leg, and a laceration on my forehead. Additionally, I spent several days in a coma. Several weeks later, I was still trying to figure out how to get rid of Susan and her grip on me.

I came down with a severe asthma attack. This one drove me into the ICU of PMH on a ventilator for several days. That morning, I got up, was in significant distress, and stopped breathing. What I am about to say was told by my attending Emergency Room Physician, "ERP," when I recovered about a week later.

The ERP, whom I will call Dr. John, a Jamaican ER Intern, told me they worked on me aggressively to restart my heart beating again, but it failed five times. The ERP told me I was dead, but he decided to try again because of my youth. On the sixth attempt, which is rare, my heart started beating again. I was immediately rushed to the ICU and placed on a ventilator. After several days in the ICU, I was transferred to the Private Medical Ward (PMW) of PMH.

Dr. John came to visit me at the PMW. He pulled up a chair to my bedside and said, "Mr. Antonio, I do not know what it was, but something in me told me to try again to revive you, and here you are today." He told me that Almighty God had a particular assignment for me, and it was not my time to leave this earth yet. I was emotionally overwhelmed, and I could not stop thanking Him. When Dr. John left, I prayed and could not stop thanking Almighty God for extending His gift of life to me for another day.

It was all because of His love and mercy that He gave me another opportunity to be a part of this earth and His unconditional love and grace that He had afforded me to testify on how great and awesome He is and that all the glory and praise goes to Him. Through all of this, I have learnt to have unshakeable faith in my creator, the Almighty God above, and that can never change. I have been able to testify to His miracles in my life and hope that this testimony will encourage and help whoever reads this book to understand God is real, truthfully real.

I was discharged from PMH, and PMW a few days later, and as the Doctor whom I will call Dr. Ferguson, was letting me go home, I realised I had a sore throat. I was given some medicine to gurgle to clear up the hoarseness in my throat.

When I got home, I used the treatment, but it only inflamed my throat and closed off my airway. I was rushed from Susan's house to the ER at PMH in the afternoon traffic. I was told it took approximately four minutes to become brain-dead, but I know it took me longer in a private vehicle to get to the hospital.

God is so awesome that I am grateful. I was rushed to the theatre at PMH for the doctor to do an emergency tracheotomy. I was told from the cardiac arrest earlier that I had while the doctors were trying to intubate me that the tube was too big; it damaged my vocal cords and throat and that I needed throat surgery to correct the problem. I was transferred to the ICU from the operating theatre and spent a few days there.

When I regained consciousness in the ICU, I was approached by a doctor whom I would call Dr. James. He was trying to get my permission to do my surgery. When I arrived in the ER, I could remember the doctor holding this big needle, and he was telling me to hold my breath while he stuck that needle in my neck. The first attempt when he stuck me failed because I coughed, and all the medicine spouted through my neck.

He immediately told me to hold my breath so he could punch me again. When he did, it worked because he knocked me out, and they rushed me to the operating theatre. They inserted a tube in my throat and told me that a tracheotomy was done for me to breathe. I had this heavy stainless-steel object inserted in my throat for me to breathe.

Dr. James was an Ear, Nose, and Throat Specialist. He said that I needed that surgery from a well-experienced ENT Specialist because my throat and voice box were damaged. He said it depends on whom I decide to do my surgery. I may never talk again. Dr. James constantly tried to convince me to do the surgery, but I explained I would like to get a second opinion. I asked him to refer me to someone he knows who could give me that second opinion. I battled with Dr. James until he finally gave me the referral letter to allow me to travel to Miami to Jackson Memorial Hospital "JMH" to get that second opinion.

I travelled to Miami and visited JMH, where I met an elderly white doctor with grey hair. When he saw me, he started dancing and smiled at me. He said, "I retired today and I'm so happy." He said, "Mr. Antonio, I have someone to whom I will introduce to you. He is young, learned, and an excellent ENT specialist. You would be in good hands." The elderly doctor, whom I refer to as Dr. Sands, told me that he would still examine me and let the young Dr., whom I will call Dr. Brown, also examine me and then compare notes.

After both examinations, they explained they had arrived at the same diagnosis or conclusion. Dr. Sands then turned me over to Dr. Brown and said, "Mr. Antonio, you are in good hands." Dr. Brown explained to me I would need to have three separate surgeries to repair my throat, my voice box, and my vocal cords. Everything was explained in detail, and he sent me back to Nassau, The Bahamas, for about a month.

After a month, I had to go back to Miami, Florida, where I had the first of three surgeries done. It took about eighteen months to have all three surgeries done and to be able to speak again. All went well, as Dr. Brown had indicated, and the rest was history. I was able to talk and live life normally.

This was another one of my Great Master, The Almighty God's miracles in my life. I have all faith and trust in Him that He was always with me. He would never leave nor forsake me because I was His child, and I continued to honour, glorify, and praise Him for His mighty works. God is awesome!

Susan went to Miami with me for the first two surgeries and was still intimate with me at every opportunity. After the last surgery, after a year and a half, I had an appointment to remove the tracheotomy from my neck because I could breathe normally, and everything was fine. I made a quick trip to the Doctor at JMH, and the tube was removed from my neck. After that, everything was fine, and I returned to Nassau, Bahamas, and resumed my everyday life. I still could not break away from Susan. I was whipped because, in her presence, I could not say no, so our saga continued.

I sometimes sat down, contemplating how she almost killed me, but there was a stronghold that would not let me go. I knew it was her because she borrowed my car and she admitted to me that she did things to me to keep me in her life and she told me that if she could not have me, nobody will. She told me that in her life she never met a man who treated her the way I did.

CHAPTER THREE

Troubles & Trials With Susan

After several months back to normal, Susan invited me to her apartment for a sleepover. I knew what that entailed, but I could not say no. I was whipped any time I was in her presence. I had no power to say no, I just had to give in to her advances. It was the usual; we bathed and spent intimate moments together.

The following day at about 8:00 a.m. Susan touched me gently and told me that she was going out for about an hour, and being half awake after a few intimate moments the night before, I said okay.

After an hour and a half had passed, the telephone rang and woke me up. The lady on the other end of the phone asked, "Is this Darren?" I said yes, and she said, "You do not know me, but your girlfriend just left my shop, and when she arrives home, I need you to borrow her car and come and see me. I will give you the directions to find my shop."

The lady was located on Balliou Hill Road in the Central part of Nassau. She gave me the directions, and when Susan arrived home, I allowed her to settle in for about fifteen minutes. Then I asked her to lend me her car to make a quick run. Susan said it was okay, and she gave me the keys. She entered the bed, and we made love before I left to see the strange lady who had called me earlier.

I followed the directions and drove in front of the lady's store. The building had some apartments on top and a food store at the bottom. She told me to walk inside the food store, and there was an open door on the right as I walked into the building. Walk through that door to a semi-dark room, went right in, and took a seat.

As I walked into the room, the lady whom I wished to call Mother Fox was sitting at a table far off in the room. She told me to have a seat, and I did as she requested. Mother Fox told me to look at what was before me and tell her what I saw. I told her I saw a list and some money on the table. She told me to pick up the list and read it. When I picked it up and began to read it, it had four requests. The first was to kill Margo, the second was that we get married, the third was that we have children, and the last was to keep me away from my family.

The first request hit me like a ton of bricks because I would have felt incredibly guilty if that had happened. This was very sobering for me. Mother Fox asked me if I had ever eaten from Susan, and I said no. I told her that I was brought up never to eat from people. She said that was good and probably why I am still alive.

Susan was a fatal attraction because, I can recall, sometimes, when we were intimate afterwards, she liked to cuddle and play with my private parts. She would always ask me if they belonged to her, and I would say yes to please her, but I realised later that it appeared that it did something to her brain. Susan would always tell me she belonged to me. Mother Fox told me that when she was paid to do a job, she always did her job. She said, "Darren, I would have liked to do my job, but for some reason, I cannot touch you." She told me, "You are covered. You are a decent young man who is caught up with a wicked young lady. You should run away from her as soon as possible because she is not suitable for you."

After I had the meeting with Mother Fox, I understood that Susan wanted Margo dead. This meant war for me, and a real concern as I had Margo on my mind - how I had put her life in danger just through my foolishness. I had to come up with a strategy.

I started thinking and planning how to get out of this relationship and get Susan out of my life so Margo could be safe. Margo did not deserve what I had brought on her. Someone trying to kill her out of pure jealousy because she loved me. I visited Susan daily and acted normal so she would not notice a change in me. I picked up the Bible daily and prayed that the Lord, God Almighty, would remove Susan from my life.

I began warfaring, praying consistently without ceasing, asking God to get me out of this and promised that once He did, I would change my life and His precepts would guide my every path.

I started reducing the days that I spent with her. If I saw her seven days a week, I would cut it down to six, find an excuse to cut it down, then five, etc. I continued praying nonstop, sincerely, and genuinely from my heart, knowing that God sees our hearts and hears the prayers of the broken hearts and faithful who truly repent of their iniquities and adulterous ways.

The Lord God, in His infinite mercies, heard my cry. He answered my prayers and delivered me. One day, a friend called me and told me that Susan had done something at work involving money, resulting in her dismissal from her job. He also said she left Nassau and moved to another island after changing her surname. Susan never called or explained anything to me; she just disappeared.

The Bible assures us we can approach God and His throne of Grace, seeking His Mercies. In 1 John 5:14-15, it reads, "This is the confidence we have in approaching God: that if we ask anything according to his will, he hears us. And if we know he hears us, whatever we ask, we know that we have what we asked of him." This is my assurance that I was forgiven by a God who loves me unconditionally.

When you pray unceasingly to our God Almighty, He always answers your prayers. The Lord God is genuine and authentic, and His Word is truth. I have been through many troubles and trials, and the Lord has been with me every step of the way. I will continue to thank and glorify His name throughout my life.

He has done many miracles in my life, knowing and unknowingly. He has protected me and guided me all my life. I belong to Him, the Most High, and have long ago accepted His son Jesus Christ's gift of salvation that He came on this earth to bring for us. His son, Jesus Christ, came on this earth to give us the gift of free salvation. Jesus was beaten, crucified, died, buried and resurrected, and now sits at the Father's right hand until the appointed time of judgment.

Despite all the trouble and trials with Susan, I have realised that sometimes our ancestors, guardians, parents, grandparents, and great-grandparents commit certain sins in their lives and are passed on to the third and fourth generations. However, the Lord is still in control, and He sometimes puts us through these trials and tribulations to build our character and to strengthen and mould us into His image.

Margo and I separated peacefully, and she was doing very well. She is now happily married with a few children, and I think she is a deaconess or reverend in her church. I telephoned her recently, and we had a lovely conversation, and I am happy for her.

I forgot to mention that I had successful surgeries when my throat was damaged; however, the right side of my vocal cords was permanently damaged — only the left side functions.

CHAPTER FOUR

Growth Amid Adversity
~ How Trials Shape Faith

In this life, you have to accept the Lord Jesus Christ's gift of salvation and ask Him to align your thoughts with His thoughts, renew your mind and heart daily, and remove the scales from your eyes so that you can see the things that the Almighty God wants and needs you to see. Ask Him to renew your heart and help you not to hold no malice against any man, be at peace with all humankind but at war with their vices and ask the Lord to give you a forgiving heart.

Ask the Holy Spirit to help you learn how to love your enemies and be kind to them. Ask Him to help you be caring, loving, empathetic, and kind. Ask the Holy Spirit to give you supernatural wisdom, knowledge, and understanding with a great measure of discernment and discretion so you can navigate this life and fulfil the Great God Almighty's purpose for your life.

Once you have changed your life, ask the Lord God Almighty to wash your sins away. You ask Him (God), through His son Jesus Christ, to invite the Holy Spirit to guide and direct your daily path. Satan is out there trying to kill, steal and destroy humanity because he knows His fate, eternally condemned, so he needs company to join him in hell. He is cunning and evil, using every device to distract you from reading — God's Word. Many people are distracted by mobiles, computers, and other things to keep them from constantly reading the Word of God so that they can get to know their maker on a personal level.

Once you have accepted the Lord Jesus Christ as your Saviour, he (Satan) will fight you with everything he has, and his primary tool is deception. He would attack you through your health, finances, marriage, family, and any weaknesses that you have. He sometimes sends people into your life to destroy you. So, you must be vigilant all the days of your life when he comes around like a prowler with his schemes. You must bind him with the blood of your Saviour, Jesus Christ. It would be best if you continued to restrain him from your health, finances, family, marriage, home, and weaknesses continuously.

After all these events, one evening, I visited my eldest sister, Jay. While visiting her, I developed a headache that evening around 9:00 p.m. so I asked her for some painkillers to alleviate the pain, and she went inside her room and brought me this tablet. I did not take note of the tablet; I just took it with some water. I went home and slept for a few hours because I had to work at midnight.

I arrived at work shortly after midnight, relieved my colleagues, and took over the shift. I was a senior control room operator, sitting at my desk doing my night work. As time passed, I started to feel this strange tingling in my body, which felt like a familiar feeling I had before. I put down my pen and thought fast, and something told me to stretch out my arm with a fist and look at my knuckles, and that is what I did.

My hands swelled to the point where I could not see my knuckles, and I had to act fast because I realised I was allergic to whatever my sister Jay had given me as a painkiller. I went into my supervisor's office and told him I had to leave to go to the hospital immediately. I explained what had happened, and he said he could not let me go because it was almost 2:00 a.m., and there was no one to replace me.

I had a co-worker and a friend whom I would call Bridgette. I called her and quickly explained my case, and she told me she was coming right away. I did not tell my supervisor once I got Bridgette's confirmation that she was coming. I got in my car and immediately drove to Doctor's Hospital. I was moving so fast that I probably arrived in about fifteen minutes. I was swollen by the time I arrived at the hospital. The emergency doctor asked me how I got to the hospital, and I told him I drove there. He told me I should have called the ambulance, and I told him I might have died waiting in the ambulance. He told me my throat could have closed up, and anything could have happened to me. Immediately, I was seen. An IV was placed into my veins with medication, and I was then transferred to the ICU. I was swollen with lots of big boils that burst. I had spots all over and spent about five days in the ICU. My body, during that whole time, changed skin literally. The thoughts that were going through my mind were I was going to make it to the hospital to get medical attention and I was going to be just fine because My Saviour was with me. I was not afraid because fear did not enter my mind.

My sister Jay, who gave me the painkillers, had Motrin and Bactrim in the same bottle, and she gave me Bactrim for Motrin. I am highly allergic to Bactrim, and the doctor advised me that if something like this ever happened again, I may not survive.

I recognised that tingling sensation because I had a chest infection a few years before and had Bactrim. That was the first time I had that experience, but it was okay. I always wore a medic alert bracelet on my left wrist. My sister Jay apologised repeatedly for that mistake, and my supervisor, whom I will call Mo, was apologetic for not acting on this matter. I dodged another life-threatening battle with the help of the Holy Spirit, leading the way with the quick decisions made for me to survive.

In March 2019, I started experiencing back pain, which worsened as time passed. I went to the spine specialist and did an MRI, which revealed that one of my lower vertebrae was slightly out of place. He told me that I could correct it with exercise and diet, which I was doing. He gave me some painkillers, but the pain became progressively worse. I battled with the aches and pains and then came the pandemic.

I did everything imaginable not to catch COVID-19, but in September 2020, I contracted it from a co-worker at BPL. I will call him Henry. Henry and I were in the office one Monday afternoon, and he appeared sick. He was wearing a mask and kept coughing. Henry's facemask kept dropping off his face, and I got furious and asked him why you came to work if you are sick. He denied being sick.

About two days later, Henry was diagnosed with COVID-19. I had called in sick a day earlier because my back was hurting me, and one of my colleagues called to notify me that Henry tested positive for COVID-19. I felt good because I was wearing a facial mask, but a few times, I pulled it down to talk on the telephone, and I am almost sure that is where I caught that terrible germ.

Henry was diagnosed on Wednesday, and I was fine, or so I thought, until Saturday of the same week, when I developed a severe headache and a runny nose like a faucet. I took some Panadol, which did not help. I ran some warm water over my face and nose and took some nose drops to stop the runny nose, but that only helped a little. I went to bed around 9:00 p.m. that night and woke up around 4:00 a.m. that Sunday morning with a bad headache, runny nose, and unbearable feelings. I told my wife we needed to go to the emergency room immediately, which we did.

CHAPTER FIVE

After The Storm, The Silver Lining

After Susan, Margo and I parted ways. I was not looking to engage in any relationship. I learned from both relationships and vowed that if I ever got involved in another relationship, it would have to be like someone with similar characteristics to Margo. Someone very loving, loyal, caring, empathetic, happy, friendly with an unquenchable thirst for God, one who prayed a lot.

I worked shifts comprising 8-4, 4-12, and 12-8, and on occasions when I was able, I would pick up my eldest niece, who attended Success Training College on Bernard Road, where she attended evening classes and took her home. Several times, I offered her friend Colette a ride because she lived close by. During our rides, I did not talk while they conversed.

As the months passed and December approached, it was time for BEC's annual Christmas Ball, which was held on the 18th. I wanted to go but did not have a date, so I dropped the idea of going one evening to my niece while dropping her home.

A couple of days later, I dropped Colette home and was about to drop my niece home. Jokingly I blurted out, "Why don't you ask your friend Colette to accompany me to the BEC Christmas Ball if she is not involved with anyone." It was just a joke, and I was not even looking for a reply.

A few days later, after dropping Colette home, my niece told me that Colette was not involved with anyone and had agreed to accompany me to the Christmas Ball if she was going. I was elated because I wanted to attend that Christmas Ball. I picked up Colette first on the night of the Ball because she lived closer to me. On our drive to collect my niece, she was well-dressed but reticent during the short drive to my niece. Upon arriving at my niece's home, Colette went inside and waited for her because she was not dressed when we arrived. The wait took longer than expected, so I went inside to see what was taking them so long; in my quest to understand the delay. I was greeted by my niece, who said my sister Jay forbade her to go. She was unhappy, but encouraged Colette to go because she was already dressed.

Several minutes later, Colette agreed, and we went to the Christmas Ball. We used that time to talk, which we never did. Surprisingly, we had a great time and spoke regularly, spending hours and hours conversing on the telephone up to the wee hours of the morning. It started from a few minutes to half an hour a day and up to several hours a day. We became friends, and several months later, we started going out and becoming better acquainted. We did our movie nights and dinners, and she frequently invited me over for Sunday dinners, which took me a while to get used to. As previously mentioned, eating from people was a no-no. Eventually, I gave in and enjoyed the home-cooked meals with her family when invited. Some Sundays, when I had to work, she would bring the Sunday dinner to BEC for me.

Other than home, Colette's aunt, where she resided, was the only place where I would eat. Her family accepted me, but her aunt was like a drill sergeant at first; she asked many questions to find out who I was and what my family was besides my intentions.

Her mother was kind, very easy-going and pleasant to speak with, and her father was quiet and smiled often; both accepted me into the family. Once I passed the approval test, I was invited more and more to have dinner and always came and waited inside, especially when I had to pick up Colette for date nights, with open arms as part of the family. One thing that drew me close to her aunt was that she espoused cleanliness and constantly cleaned. She was interested in getting to know me.

Colette is a person who works hard for what she wants and strives for growth in everything she does. She is selfless and always puts people first before her needs.

When choosing a partner, I placed a lot of emphasis on attitude, a caring personality, being very loving, trusting, and being concerned about myself and others. Also, loyalty and honesty played a vital role in my decision. I saw these and many more characteristics that she possessed with which I could live. She was attractive, but these are secondary things to me. In terms of falling in love, it did not happen overnight; by choice, I decided to love her. It grew incrementally over time.

We became acquaintances, then friends, and eventually we got serious. I began to notice that she had some of the same characteristics as Margo, and this is what I was easily attracted to. She had a peaceful personality. She was kind, caring, loving, and loyal in ways that I could live with, very pleasant. These were some of the positive characteristics that attracted me to her, along with getting to know her as a friend and taking things slowly. Also, she grew into a God-fearing woman. It was evident that she loved me because when she got in my presence, her face always lit up. It was a pleasure for her to be in my company and for me, likewise.

We are both Catholics and in terms of raising a family, we have similar ideologies. Our relationship was unique, and I proposed to her two years later. We were married at St. Anselm's Catholic Church, Colette's church. Everything was paid for, and we owed nobody a cent on our wedding. Colette's boss and his company then paid for our honeymoon, a seven-day Caribbean Cruise on the Paradise Ship, as a wedding gift. Everything went well.

We were now property owners, having purchased a piece of land east of New Providence, where we were blessed to have her father and uncle as contractors to build our home. Colette's father and uncle completed our home and both are now deceased. May God continue to bless their souls. God was with us because everything went so smoothly. Today, we have been married for twenty-three years, having been together for about thirty-one years, and we have a pretty good marriage. Thanks be to God. We have two children, a son, fifteen, and a daughter, twenty-two.

CHAPTER SIX

"One Thing After The Other"

We arrived at Doctor's Hospital around 4:30 a.m. I was registered right away and placed in cubicle 7. The doctor questioned me about COVID-19, but I told him I had not travelled for a couple of years and nobody in my home had COVID-19. I also told him that I used to have sinuses one time ago, and he placed an IV on me with pain medications and treated me for sinusitis. I was in the hospital emergency room until after 11:00 a.m. that morning and then later discharged with some painkillers and nose spray, and overall, I felt good. My headache and runny nose went away, and I felt good.

The following morning, I was off work and sitting on my bed, and a thought came to me. I absorbed every news story about COVID-19 and was thoroughly knowledgeable about the symptoms and what to do if I contracted that germ. The thought was, you have some Dettol in your bathroom; put it to your left nostril and see if you can smell it. I went into the bathroom, opened the Dettol, and placed it on my left nostril, but I could not smell anything. I immediately told myself that you have some bleach in the kitchen cupboard, and I got it and placed it under my right nostril. I did that and could not smell anything. I was in denial because I still did not think I had COVID-19. In the days that followed, it was like hell on earth. All of this time, my back was getting worse and here comes COVID-19.

I had lost my sense of smell and taste in the coming days and then my appetite. I weighed slightly over 200 pounds before COVID-19 and lost my appetite. I started to lose weight. I woke up with these terrible feelings and headaches and slept intermittently. I did not go to the hospital because my breathing was alright, but I thought I would die. My wife brought me breakfast, lunch and dinner, and I could eat none of it. I dropped over three weeks from 200 to 151 pounds and could not smell or taste for over two weeks. I lost my appetite for about three weeks. Inside, my mouth and lips were full of soars. I looked like a skeleton. I drank water several times daily and occasionally a can of apple or orange juice.

I had a tiny pharmacy home, and I treated myself. My wife came inside the bedroom one morning to bring some breakfast, and I refused to eat it, but the look on her face said that if I did not start eating, I would not make it. I started eating everything on site the next day while I treated myself with medication. I took 500 mg of Amoxicillin every eight hours for infection, 20 mg of prednisone for inflammation, Pradaxa for my back for blood clots and 500 mg of Panadol for headaches.

I started eating everything and anything and dragged myself out of bed to go to the carport to catch the sunlight. As I drank plenty of water daily, I began to gain a little strength, and for the sores in my mouth, lips, and throat, I used Hydrogen Peroxide to treat the sore, and in about several hours, the soars disappeared. Hydrogen Peroxide is very good.

I was battling with COVID-19 for approximately a month. I lost my sense of smell and taste for over two weeks and my appetite for over three weeks, and with all of this battling, my spine was getting worse. I took Tramadol 1000 mg every eight hours for the excruciating pain that I was experiencing almost all day. I only got a little relief when I was asleep.

As I continued to eat and drink, my strength increased, and in early October 2020, I felt good. My taste and smell were still pretty messed up when they returned, but I struggled for weeks. After I got over COVID-19, I got tested, and it came back negative, and I was ecstatic. It was one down and one to go. I still had severe back pains through all these troubles and trials. Those pains were so intense that I was on heavy painkillers. As the pain worsened, it started to affect my right leg. I was on and off attending work until I was bedridden. This pain was so intense that I could only cry and take my painkillers to return to sleep when I awoke. I went to my spine specialist, and he ran some tests and did another MRI, which was pretty bad.

In early December, I saw him, and he showed me my MRI. It showed that one of my lower vertebrae had come entirely out of place and was sitting on my nerve, which was why my whole body was in pain. I was in so much pain that when I went to urinate; it was as if someone had a vice grip on my testicles; that was how excruciating the pain was.

My spine specialist, I wish to call Dr. G, sat me and my wife down and explained the pros and cons of having that type of surgery. After talking to us, he also opened up to questions we had. After our appointment with him, he asked us to sit down with a surgeon who would be on his team for a consultation. I wanted a second opinion, but with the pandemic, all the travelling issues, and unbearable pain, I decided with my wife to have the surgery locally. The date was set for Monday, 15th February, 2021 at 9:00 a.m. I was told to check in that Sunday at 1:00 p.m. in the Private Surgical Ward of PMH on the 14th of January, which I did.

On Monday at 8:00 a.m., I was taken to the recovery room and prepped for my surgery. I had certain negative people casting doubts about my doctor, Dr. G. Some people said that I would probably end up paralysed or dead, but I trusted my God, kept a positive mental attitude, and knew that I would be just fine.

I was transferred to the operating theatre at about 8:55 a.m. The anaesthesiologist inquired whether I was alright, and I said yes. I said to my God, "I will live and not die." She placed a mask on my face at 9:00 a.m., and within seconds, I was asleep. I spent the whole day in surgery and awoke at 5:00 p.m. I was immediately given an injection for pain, and I went back to sleep.

At about midnight, I finally woke up in the Private Surgical Ward with two bags of drip, dripping simultaneously. I was administered another injection and was fast asleep within minutes. The surgery was a success, and I was doing great. I had vertebrae removed and two titanium plates with screws inserted in my lower back, and I thank God every day for His miracle. After going through all these troubles again and trials, I was doing fantastic for a few months.

I woke up on a Tuesday morning in May and was fine when I went to bed, but I woke up feeling as if I was going to die. This was at the height of the pandemic. My wife was working three days at home and two at the office, and my daughter, who attends the University of The Bahamas, was doing her classes online, and my son, who attends St. Anne's School, was doing his classes online.

My wife was getting ready for work, and my children's classes started probably around 8:00 a.m. for my son and maybe 9:00 a.m. for my daughter. My wife got ready, and as she was leaving, I told her I was not feeling well and would be alright. She left for work, and the bad feelings persisted. I fell asleep for about two hours and felt worse than before.

Like any caring family, my wife and kids try to understand why I go through so much. They prayed for God to deliver me from the trials I had faced. Yes, they were afraid and sometimes got emotional, but they tried to be strong for each other and me as we faced these challenging journeys.

My family believes I am stronger than I look, as I handle things better than most. I constantly remind them not to get down or feel depressed but to be reminded that God was always in control, even when we do not understand and that God was not done with me as yet.

I wrestled in my mind if I would attempt to go to the hospital or lie there, hoping that the feelings would subside. Around afternoon, I heard a small voice say Darren, go to the hospital, and shortly afterwards, another small voice said go back to sleep.

I always listen to that first still small voice in my ears, and that is what I did. I attempted to put my clothes on, but I was so weak, and I fell back into bed. It was as if something or someone was trying to keep me at home. I said a small prayer, "Lord, I am going to the hospital, but I need you to get me there safely because I don't think I can drive my vehicle."

I made a third attempt to get my clothes on and succeeded. I stopped by my daughter's room and then by my son's room and I told them I was headed to the hospital because I did not feel well. They wished me well, and I slowly got in the garage, opened my jeep door, and sat in my jeep for a few minutes collecting myself. At this time, it was nearly 1:00 p.m., and I started the vehicle, and I was on my way.

Traffic was tight, but I arrived in the Doctor's Hospital parking lot around 1:30 p.m. Honestly, I do not know how I got there, but God took the wheel and drove me safely into the Hospital's parking lot. I sat in the parking lot for about five minutes, thanking God and collecting myself to walk to the ER. I strolled to the ER door around the front of the hospital.

As I entered the door, two ladies were sitting at the desk near to it, and as I entered, they greeted me. One of them, who I learned later as a nurse, asked me why I came to the hospital. I told her I was weak and feeling very bad, and she immediately began registering me. The lady got a wheelchair for me to sit in, rolled me to the right side of the desk, and began to take my vital signs. As she moved me to the other side, we casually talked, and I was very conscious about what was happening.

The nurse placed the blood pressure apparatus on my arm to check my blood pressure, and I heard her say he had no blood pressure under her breath. She said, "Let me try again because I did not get any reading." The nurse squeezed the air out of the blood pressure cuff and then tried to get a blood pressure. I heard the nurse under her breath say he had no blood pressure.

She immediately went to the wall where a telephone was and called the ER. I could hear her speaking to the person on the other side of the phone that she had a patient out there, and he had no blood pressure. I assumed that the person on the other end of the phone told her to try one more time, and she did. She said I am not getting a blood pressure, so we have to go. She did not tell me that but talked under her breath, and I could hear everything.

The nurse turned me around and rushed me into ER cubicle #3. I saw about five to six people in their medical outfits waiting for me. The nurse parked me near the bed, and two people assisted me on the bed. I had one individual putting on an IV in my hand, another person putting on a heart monitor, and another person putting on a heart monitor. I had one individual who took off my shirt, and I was lying down. I lifted my head, and I saw zero on the monitor.

One person, whom I assumed was a doctor, gave me two big white tablets, and she told me, Mr. Antonio, these are two Anacin tablets, and I want you to chew them up and swallow them quickly. I chewed up the tablets and I devoured them. Then she gave me a small tablet and told me that this was a nitroglycerin tablet to put under my tongue and would melt in seconds. She also said that this tablet's purpose is to open up all the vessels going to my heart to carry blood. I placed the pill under my tongue, which melted as she said.

I had another person pushing medicine in the IV that was in my hand. All the while, from their conversations, they were shocked that I had never lost consciousness. After pushing and administering all those medications, I looked up at the monitor and saw my blood pressure and pulse gradually increasing. The medical team watched me and the monitor as my heart rate and blood pressure increased. They could not find words to explain what had happened to me, and I was so relaxed and comfortable that I felt unafraid.

Once they stabilised my vital signs, blood was drawn and sent to the lab. I had an EKG, Eco-cardiogram and Ex-Rays done on me all day. The doctors told me that all of my tests came back normal and that they did not have a reason for what had happened to me. I lay in my bed praying for hours, thanking God for sparing my life and for His gift of life. It was a long prayer and talk I had with my God. He has once again proven to me that He exists and is always there to take good care of His children.

I have proven that for all the years I have lived, God is true and that He is the truth, and there is none like Him, and there will never be any like Him. He has been King of Kings and Lord of Lords from ancient days and is from every lasting to everlasting. I am eternally proud to have Him as my Lord and Master, and I will always give Him all the praise and glory for creating and loving me unconditionally and for extending His grace and mercy to me.

I have always embraced His power and faith in Him despite adversity. I believe in my God; He has control of my life, and I will serve Him for eternity.

CHAPTER SEVEN
Learning To Trust God In Trials

When trusting the Almighty God in trials and tribulations, you have to address Him for your specific needs. One of the faith-based verses that has impressed me is in the New Testament, James 5: 13-16. In this verse, He asks you, "If any among you are suffering. Let him pray. Is anyone cheerful? Let him sing Psalms. Is anyone among you sick? Let him call for the church elders and let them pray over him with oil in the name of the Lord. And the prayer of faith will save the sick, and the Lord will raise him. And if he has committed sins, he will be forgiven. Confess your trespasses to one another and pray for one another so that you may be healed. The effective, fervent prayer of a righteous man avails much."

The believer will have to pray constantly without ceasing and continue to be patient because the Almighty God works in His time. Once you have as for your specific needs, trust Him and have faith in Him that your request will be met.

If you have genuinely requested and have accepted the Lord Jesus Christ as your personal Saviour and according to what you ask in His Word, the Master will grant you healing according to His will or His intent for your life. He cannot lie, go back or change His words. He is the Word, and the Word is truth.

In trusting God through trials and tribulations, we must focus on Him, not on what we are experiencing. We have to use this time, although challenging. It is hard to concentrate on anything other than your present condition, but God knows your heart. When you cannot speak, the burdens are unbearable; they seem too heavy to carry; this is when we lean on Him as we have never done before and our faith, which the Bible tells us moves mountains as small as a mustard seed.

Faith helps us to contact God; it allows us to hold fast and strong in trying times, in times of despair, and when there is no one or nothing else to trust in or rely on. God is faithful and just and does what He says He will. His Word reminds us in Isaiah 55:11, "So shall my word be that goes forth from My mouth; It shall not return to Me void, But it shall accomplish what I please, And it shall prosper in the thing for which I sent it."

Our faith is what helps us to tarry and navigate through the darkness. It creates a light beam when the darkness seems so thick and foggy. It helps us to trust the one who leads us, holding on to Him and allowing Him to guide every step without us fumbling mindlessly. Faith helps us to manifest what may seem not within reach; it helps us to be persistent, sincere, and unwavering in our belief in a God that will open the heaven and pour out a blessing, healing and unmerited favour upon us.

Faith helps us rely on God no matter how long and bleak things look. What we see in front of us or how things may seem. With God, things change instantly, and our situations miraculously become a path of our journey where we can speak of the goodness of God. During our faith walk, our trials stop when things change. It means we trust Him even more because we know when He delivered us.

Just like seasons, trials and tribulations do not last beyond its season. We are strengthened; we become warriors, resilient, and steadfast because of God's promises. Isaiah 41:10 calls us to "Fear not, for I am with you; be not dismayed, for I am your God; I will strengthen you, I will help you, I will uphold you with my righteous right hand." There have been many moments before going up to preach that I face the giant of discouragement. God is real and promises never to leave or forsake us. Therefore, we are to be encouraged to believe and trust Him and allow our faith to take root, fueling it with His Word, knowing that the strength of God is always within us and within our reach.

CHAPTER EIGHT
Inspiring Others To Believe

Inspiring others is not always easy, especially when they cannot see beyond their difficulties. However, it takes special gifts of compassion, empathy, love, time, and the ability to tell your story of how God moved, directed, and showed up when there was no way out of the desert; no superpower in the world could have done what only God did for you. He took the scale of my eyes, revealed who He was, opened Himself, and I could see His unconditional love, which manifested and transformed me. All this was possible through the Holy Spirit, who influenced my belief and allowed me to increase my faith, which helped me believe in Him through your journey.

When inspiring others to believe in the Lord Jesus Christ, you must encourage them first to establish a relationship with God the Almighty – to cultivate a relationship with Him. In Jeremiah 29: 12-13, it says, "Then you will call upon me and come and pray to me, and I will hear you. You will seek and find me when you seek me with all your heart."

When you truly seek the Lord with all your heart, He will make Himself available to you. He would accommodate you, which could be your sincerity, the beginning of an external relationship between you both. You must never forget that the Almighty God comes first and does not share His glory with anyone or anything. According to Matthew 6:24, it says, "No one can serve two masters; for either he will hate the one and love the other, or he will be devoted to the one and despise the other. You cannot serve God and mammon." Whatever we put before God is what we worship and is considered our master, e.g. worldly possessions, status or money.

God wants us to glorify Him, be obedient, worship, and receive His unconditional love and, by extension, His grace and mercy when we accept

His son, Jesus Christ, who suffered and paid a hefty price for our salvation. In the book of Matthew 22: 37-38, the first of the gospels, the word states, "And he said to Him, you shall love the Lord your God with all your heart and with all your soul and with all your mind. This is the great and first commandment". We are to honour and lift Him before any earthly possession.

As you read His Word daily, you develop that relationship which can only come with spending time with Him, trusting Him and seeking Him with your whole heart, mind and spirit. Romans 10:17 brings it home, "So then faith comes by hearing and hearing by the word of God". As a new believer, you can only grow more in faith if you constantly stay in the Word as often as possible so the Holy Spirit can be activated in you and can transform you by dominating your thoughts according to God's will because He was left as our helper when the Lord ascended into heaven.

As our helper, the Holy Spirit works on the Almighty God's behalf to do more incredible things than Him. The Holy Spirit is your guide, teacher, protector, provider, and comforter; He is your everything.

CHAPTER NINE
Faith Above All Things

What is Faith? Hebrews 11:1 states, "Now faith is the assurance of things hoped for, the conviction of things not seen". In other words, I have confidence and trust in my God and His promises, although I have not physically seen Him.

I am a recipient of His works or miracles, known and unknown throughout my life from the day I came into this world to the present day. Almighty God, His Son, Jesus Christ, was sent to earth to save us from eternal damnation with all of my being. I have a very strong trust, conviction and confidence in my Creator, the Great God Almighty. Ephesians 2 8:10 states, "For it is by grace you have been saved, through faith and this is not from yourselves, it is the gift of God not by works, so that no one can boast. For we are God's handiwork, created in Christ Jesus to do good works, which God prepared us to do." So, all the rewards of glory go to God Almighty.

The more we seek Him, the more we want to know Him, rely on and trust Him. Our confidence grows, and then our faith becomes so unshakeable that it never wavers, no matter what comes our way. God is sovereign and king. We should know that we need Him. It is our duty to call upon Him, ask and go to Him with everything before we take it elsewhere.

When our faith is unshakeable, we do not need to go to man to speak of our challenges. We go directly to our source, Almighty God. Our faith helps us seek and talk to Him through prayer and petition, allowing the Holy Spirit to guide us to be our advocate. When we do this, we release fear, worry, anxiety, and negative thinking as they relate to our problems, trials, and any tribulations that we may encounter. This is not to say that we don't think about it or that it is not on our minds, but we know that we will not face them alone and that God is behind the scenes, aligning things out, and He will be done with the situation, and we are to trust Him and the process as God's timing is always right.

Matthew 6: 26-27 puts it into context for us, "Look at the birds of the air; they do not sow or reap or store away in barns, and yet your heavenly Father feeds them. Are you not much more valuable than they? Can any one of you, by worrying, add a single hour to your life?" As God feeds and takes care of the birds of the air, He too takes care of us.

Our faith, reliance and trust in Him is what ignites the power of God to move and work within our lives. He fed the four and the five thousand, parted the Red Sea, healed and performed many miracles, and raised Lazarus from the dead. Isn't God worth putting your trust in Him? Try Him today. You have nothing to lose, but everything to gain.

Conclusion

I did not make my start in life as a saint. Even though I was raised in the Roman Catholic faith, I went to church regularly to stay out of trouble and have something meaningful to guide me in the right direction - the church. Earlier in my life, I started experiencing medical challenges and sought solutions to alleviate life-threatening challenges, and it caused me to think deeply about life and death.

Two things captured my attention. Here I am as a youth, just starting life, and I was faced with some devastating life-and-death situations. My religious background was the formation of me taking a serious interest in the Bible, even though it was inconsistent. Despite what I went through, I learned one crucial lesson that I have been taught: after all is said and done, once you repent and change your life sincerely and genuinely, you ask the Lord to cleanse your mind, heart and soul, He will wash you white as snow from all your sins and forgive them.

The key to it all is aligning your thoughts with Christ and thinking purely and righteously daily. In doing so, ask the Lord to remove the scales from your eyes and give you eagle vision to see what He needs and wants you to see and do. Ask Him to unclog your ears so you can hear what He wants you to and require you to know.

Ask Him daily to renew your heart and not allow you to hold any vibe or animosity against and with others. Always have a forgiving spirit and soul. These are God's requirements for living Christ-like, and we must live a holy and righteous life pleasing to God.

Why?" He is my Creator. He knows me better than I know myself. He knows my thoughts before I even think them and my words before I speak them. He is the King of Kings. He is the Lord of Lords from ancient days, from everlasting to everlasting. He is, and there will never be any like other than Him. He has created everything for Himself and us for His pleasure. He has proven Himself to me daily.

As we navigate these last days of Noah, we have to be aligned with God and ensure we serve God eternally in His kingdom and not lose out to that other fellow, which is eternal damnation. Why not choose a life that is eternal with our Creator?

About The Book

Life is a journey and navigating it either makes or breaks us. Some of us are strong, resilient, and brave. Some of us fold up because life is not easy. The daily pressures, stress, and challenges we sometimes face are harsh and seem unfair and unbearable.

Those who handle it do not understand but decide there are two choices: either give up or ride out the wave, remembering that everything we face is only for a season, and trouble does not last forever, but for a moment.

In Unshakeable, Darren Antonio Sr. takes the readers on a journey of lust, love, deception, wickedness, sickness, pain and faith all rolled into one. The book centers on many life-changing experiences and lessons which led Darren to a humbling point of consciousness that God is real and that when we are going through life's critical moments, whether death or life, God is always with us. This book reminds us that when we take our eyes off our problems and let God, we see miracles and the hand of God moving.

His trials started when he was a mere teen battling Asthma. He was also the black sheep and did not understand why and what was happening to him. He did not have a father or male figure that he could emulate or teach him right from wrong. These challenges plagued and disrupted his life in every area where he should have been enjoying and doing things that kids, teens and adults would do.

In this book, Darren also allowed Satan not only to tempt him but also to cause him to go off course by getting involved in a relationship, which caused him to be taken over by a sexual spirit that only God was able to deliver him from. The clutches of a woman who was black in heart and soul, and his lack of vision caused him to hurt instead of being loved, being used and being unfaithful, having had multiple relationships at the same time. He allowed the pleasures of the flesh, deception, and greed to cloud his better judgement and detour him from making wise decisions.

Eventually, he was delivered and set free by embracing faith amid adversities - unshakeable

About The Author

Darren D. Antonio, Sr. is fifty-eight, having been married to his wonderful and supportive wife, Colette B. Antonio, for the past twenty-three years. Out of this union produced two intellectual and amazing children, an adult daughter and a teen son.

As the sixth child out of seven, he was always an avid reader of anything he got his hands on: books, the Bible, newspapers, and sports magazines. Today, he still has a passion for knowledge and wisdom from God Almighty.

As a believer in Jesus Christ, he and his family worship weekly at one of the local Roman Catholic Churches in Nassau, The Bahamas. He is a lover of sports and keeps up to date with domestic and world news, especially those that align with Bible prophecies to show himself approved and to live according to the laws set out in the Bible. He and his family continue to love and serve God.

48004CB00002B/795